WHAT WAS LOST

by Steven Carl McCasland

Copyright © 2016 Steven Carl McCasland

All rights reserved.

ISBN: 1533161925
ISBN-13: 978-1533161925

Cover Photo by Samantha Mercado-Tudda

CAUTION: Professionals and amateurs are hereby warned that performance of WHAT WAS LOST *is subject to a royalty. It is fully protected under the copyright laws of the United States of America, and of all countries covered by the International Copyright Union). The professional and amateur stage performance rights may be obtained by contacting the author at steven.mccasland@gmail.com.*

WHAT WAS LOST

STEVEN CARL MCCASLAND

PRODUCTION HISTORY

What Was Lost premiered at The Dorothy Strelsin Theatre in 2014, produced by The Beautiful Soup Theater Collective with direction by the playwright. The cast was as follows:

LAURETTE TAYLOR: PennyLynn White
TENNESSEE WILLIAMS: Paul Thomas Ryan
MARGUERITE TAYLOR: Kimberly Faye Greenberg
MARGO JONES: Kristen Gehling
EDDIE DOWLING: Colin Fisher
JULIE HAYDON/RUBY: Renee Heitmann
RANDOLPH ECHOLS/FRANK MERLO: Brian Piehl

What Was Lost was revived at New York's Clarion Theatre in 2015, with direction by the playwright. The cast was as follows:

LAURETTE TAYLOR: PennyLynn White
TENNESSEE WILLIAMS: Paul Thomas Ryan
MARGUERITE TAYLOR: Kimberly Faye Greenberg
MARGO JONES: Kristen Gehling
EDDIE DOWLING: Colin Fisher
JULIE HAYDON/RUBY: Rachel Adams
RANDOLPH ECHOLS/FRANK MERLO: Brian Piehl

CHARACTERS

LAURETTE TAYLOR. 56-62. An American actress of stage and screen. Alcoholic.

TENNESSEE WILLIAMS. 33. A chain-smoking, bourbon drinking, homosexual playwright.

MARGUERITE TAYLOR. 30's. Laurette's daughter.

EDDIE DOWLING. 40's. A man of one-too-many hats. Very light in his loafers. Also plays Tom Wingfield.

MARGO JONES. 30's. A good Southern girl. Also a director and producer.

JULIE HAYDON. 30's. A tragically pretty young actress. (Actress should double as Ruby.)

RANDOLPH ECHOLS. 30. A Stage Manager. (Actor should double as Stage Manager and Frank Merlo.)

RUBY. 30's. Laurette's dresser.

FRANK. 26. Tennessee's very handsome lover. An amalgam of every man Tennessee has ever loved.

A STAGE MANAGER. 30's.

TIME AND PLACE

1939-1944. Various locations in Laurette Taylor's life. Apartments, dressing rooms, rehearsal studios, stages and watering holes.

AUTHOR'S NOTE

While *What Was Lost* is inspired by actual events, this is a work of fiction.

A / represents the moment in which the next speaker should begin to overlap. The current speaker should absolutely finish the line.

Blackouts should be avoided wherever possible. The play should keep moving fluidly between time and space.

Some doubling suggestions appear in the cast list. These may be used at the director's discretion. When a character is represented as LAURETTE/AMANDA or JULIE/LAURA, the second name is the character from "The Glass Menagerie" which they are currently playing.

Yes, the confessions are "meetings". But don't be too obvious and allow the audience discover this over the course of the play.

The play is to be performed without an intermission.

WHAT WAS LOST

SCENE 1

(LAURETTE is armed with an eye-lining pencil and staring into the mirror. It is the final performance of OUTWARD BOUND - July 22, 1939. The stage manager will be calling for places any moment.)

LAURETTE. Very wise, Laurie, very smart indeed. Very fucking wise and smart getting bombed before a final matinee. And that bastard pig fool Vincent Price with his shenanigans--

(RUBY enters with a costume.)

LAURETTE. Oh, Ruby, thank goodness. Run down and fetch me a little nip of scotch. I'm fresh out and if I'm going to get through my 255th cruise on this fucking ship with that moron Vincent Price I'm going to need just a little nip of scotch.

RUBY. It'll be your third, miss.

LAURETTE. My sixth. Stop counting.

RUBY. Allright.

LAURETTE. We're the only ones who'll know.

RUBY. Mr. Price might catch a whiff or two.

LAURETTE. My breath is better than his rotten cologne. I got through every minute of *Peg o' My Heart* thanks to a little nip of scotch. And who knew?

RUBY. No one.

LAURETTE. Go on, then.

RUBY. Allright. *(She goes.)*

LAURETTE. Vincent. Fucking. Price. *(Beat.)* What's become of you, Lady Taylor? Look at those lines across your face.

(RUBY re-enters with a drink in hand. LAURETTE takes it and drinks it down quick.)

LAURETTE. Thank you, Ruby.

RUBY. You've got two minutes, Miss Taylor.

LAURETTE. Already? *(She sighs, reaching down for a pair of heels.)* Oh, to go out there barefoot...

(She stumbles a moment, losing her balance. Beat. They're both aware how very drunk she is.)

RUBY. Do you think you should--

LAURETTE. It's a comedy. *(Beat.)* I'll get through it, Ruby, it's a comedy. Help me into these.

(RUBY kneels down and helps LAURETTE into the shoes. LAURETTE begins to leave.)

RUBY. You'll need the shawl, miss.

LAURETTE. Right.

(RUBY takes the shawl from the hook and drapes it around LAURETTE'S shoulders.)

LAURETTE. You're a gem. Do you know that, Ruby? You are a gem.

(The STAGE MANAGER pokes his head inside the door.)

WHAT WAS LOST

STAGE MANAGER. Places for Act Two, Miss Taylor.

(He's gone.)

LAURETTE. I'm bored, Ruby. I'm so very, very bored.

RUBY. I know.

(Beat. LAURETTE exits. RUBY closes the door and begins to tidy up as the lights fade to black.)

SCENE 2

(Six years later: 1944. LAURETTE'S apartment. It was once a very nice home, but it has begun to show its age. There are stacks of newspapers in an organized chaos. Many unread scripts, too. A phone somewhere has been pulled from the wall. The curtains have been taped shut. The radio is on. A waltz is playing. From a bathroom offstage, we can hear a woman humming and yadada-ing. After a moment, the sound of keys at the front door as MARGUERITE enters.)

MARGUERITE. Mom? *(Beat. With fear,)* Mother?

LAURETTE *(off)*. Be right there!

MARGUERITE. Why is it so dark?

LAURETTE *(off)*. What?

MARGUERITE. It's so dark!

(LAURETTE enters and turns off the radio.)

LAURETTE. I like it like that.

MARGUERITE. How do you get anything done?

LAURETTE. It's peaceful.

MARGUERITE. Hi.

LAURETTE. Hello.

(They embrace.)

MARGUERITE. I tried calling--

LAURETTE. I pulled it out of the wall.

MARGUERITE. But--

LAURETTE. Whenever it rang, I wanted to go to the bar and have a drink. So, I pulled it out of the wall.

MARGUERITE. When?

LAURETTE. Last week.

MARGUERITE. Have you been looking for work?

LAURETTE. It should be looking for me.

MARGUERITE. Doesn't it? *(Beat. She pulls a script off one of the piles.)* How about this one?

LAURETTE. Trash.

MARGUERITE. You've read it?

LAURETTE. Of course, I haven't read it, Marguerite. They're all trash.

MARGUERITE. How can they be trash if you haven't--

LAURETTE. Because I'm frightened. *(Beat.)* Is it necessary to force me? Is it necessary to force me to say that? It is frightening. Going out there every night. A person needs a friend out there. A person needs gin on Tuesdays and bourbon, oh, always bourbon on two-show days. A person requires it because it's frightening out there and being frightened isn't any fun.

MARGUERITE. And what happens when the money runs out? I certainly haven't got a--

LAURETTE. Don't. Don't do that. Don't assume I would ever--

MARGUERITE. Wouldn't you?

LAURETTE. No. *(Beat.)* I'd tour in stock first.

(A long silence passes.)

MARGUERITE. What happens next? *(Beat.)* Can I open up the windows? *(Beat.)* What happens next?

LAURETTE. There *is* a play...

MARGUERITE. Go on.

LAURETTE. It's good. *(Beat.)* Decent, I suppose. Sad, if you like that sort of a play. Couldn't see Vincent Price in a play like that, no...

MARGUERITE. What is it?

LAURETTE. Something new. Written by a nobody. Margo Jones is directing. She's smart.

MARGUERITE. See?

LAURETTE. They're going to Chicago first. Chicago!

MARGUERITE. So, what?

LAURETTE. Chicago is tempting. Just the thought of it makes me thirsty.

MARGUERITE. But if you like the play--

LAURETTE. It's fine.

MARGUERITE. Fine is better than decent.

LAURETTE. Some of it is quite lovely.

MARGUERITE. Well--

LAURETTE. There's a few large speeches. Those will have to go. It's been too long.

MARGUERITE. How large?

LAURETTE. Large. Beasts, even.

MARGUERITE. You'll manage.

LAURETTE. You have to start small when you first start climbing mountains, Marguerite. One doesn't simply hop onto Everest.

MARGUERITE. Call Margo.

LAURETTE. The telephone--

MARGUERITE. *(Reaching into her purse,)* Go downstairs to the payphone and call Margo. Then call the repair man and ask him to fix your telephone.

LAURETTE. Is this mad? Are we mad?

MARGUERITE. Certainly not. *(Beat.)* It's time!

LAURETTE. Chicago.

(She takes the coins and exits. Blackout.)

FIRST CONFESSION

(MARGO and TENNESSEE stand in individual pools of light.)

MARGO. Laurette, I was delighted to hear of your interest in The Gentleman Caller.

TENNESSEE. Last evening, I saw Tosca.

MARGO. It is quite a remarkable piece of writing.

TENNESSEE. I lived for art, she said.

MARGO. The young author is most certainly worthy of your attention.

TENNESSEE. I lived for love, she sang.

MARGO. You will meet Mr. Tennessee Williams at the first read-through on August the third.

TENNESSEE. Why, why, Lord, do you reward me thus?

MARGO. Please find your contract attached. Pay special attention to the clause regarding our weeks in Chicago.

TENNESSEE. What if they hate it? What if they sink in their teeth and tear it apart? What if they leave all its insides splattered across the floor? Like they did with Rose.

MARGO. Do not hesitate--

TENNESSEE. Like we did with Rose.

MARGO. --to ring with questions.

TENNESSEE. It frightens me. *(Beat.)* What happens if I confess my sins and no one is there to listen? I helped destroy her, and now I defile her. The first rehearsal is in a week.

MARGO. It has been quite some time, Laurette.

TENNESSEE. The first rehearsal is in a week. Six days to be precise. *(Beat.)* Why, Lord--

MARGO. We are all so eager to see you back on stage.

TENNESSEE. "Why do you reward me thus?"

(LAURETTE appears in a pinspot.)

LAURETTE. "We are all so eager to see you back."

MARGO. Sincerely, Margo Jones.

(TENNESSEE and MARGO exit. The pinspot grows to reveal LAURETTE standing in her apartment, holding a cup of coffee.)

LAURETTE. I read it twenty-three times. Can you believe it? Twenty. Three. Times. I stood in my bedroom and I read it. I sat on my bed and I read it. I went outside and I read it. I went to the coffeeshop and I had a cup of coffee with milk and sugar and I read it and then, would you believe, I needed to read it again so I ordered a cheese danish. *(Beat.)* "We are all so eager to see you back." Why eager? Why not happy? Why not, enthused? Why not - I don't know. Excited! Why not? *(Beat.)* Somewhere around my third bite of the danish, I realized that she was worried. And when I read it again, I could hear it. The worry in that word. She was delighted, yes, but worried. That I'd-- what? Fail? That I'd... *(Beat.)* That I'd slip? *(Beat.)* What if? It's scary out there. All those lights and, oh, the people. And a new play. A sad one, too? What if they hate it? What if I do? *(Beat.)* Slip, I mean. *(Beat.)* What, then? *(Beat.)* I think I've gone over my time. Thank-- Thank you for listening.

SCENE 3

(LAURETTE'S apartment, a few weeks later. There is a knock at the door.)

EDDIE *(off)*. Laurette?

LAURETTE. She isn't home!

EDDIE *(off)*. Miss Taylor, this is Eddie Dowling!

LAURETTE. Miss Taylor is not home.

EDDIE *(off)*. I recognize your voice, Laurette. Please open the door.

LAURETTE. You'll have to try again tomorrow, Mr. Downling.

EDDIE *(off)*. I've tried three times!

LAURETTE. Yes. You certainly are persistent.

EDDIE *(off)*. Please, if you'd just-- Just open the door, Laurette.

(Beat.)

LAURETTE. Fine. But I'm not making you any tea. *(She opens the door.)*

EDDIE. Hello.

LAURETTE. Hello.

EDDIE. May I--

LAURETTE. Yes. But leave your jacket on. You won't be here for very long, Mister...

EDDIE. Dowling.

LAURETTE. Yes. I don't take meetings at home, Mr. Dowling--

EDDIE. If I could just pick up the contracts, I'd be out of your way in--

LAURETTE. The contracts?

EDDIE. For the play, yes.

LAURETTE. The contracts...

EDDIE. I'm certain the girl brought them over--

LAURETTE. She did.

EDDIE. And you've signed them.

(Beat.)

LAURETTE. It's just that--

EDDIE. The money?

LAURETTE. No. Heavens.

EDDIE. The play.

LAURETTE. Well--

EDDIE. It's beautiful.

LAURETTE. It's sad.

EDDIE. And what's the harm in that?

LAURETTE. Sad is scary.

EDDIE. So are lots of things. Don't you think Helen Hayes gets scared?

LAURETTE. Only of the Devil Himself.

EDDIE. I know for a fact you two dined together.

LAURETTE. I know for a fact I was bored to tears.

EDDIE. Precisely why I haven't offered her the role.

LAURETTE. Did you come here to talk about Helen Hayes, Mr. Dowling, or the play? Because I've so very many things to do--

EDDIE. You might want to change out of that robe then.

(Beat.)

LAURETTE. I do comedies, Mr. Dowling. Even Peg, poor old Peg, was a comedy. People don't go to the theater to see me cry--

EDDIE. But that's just it, Laurie! May I call you Laurie? It's time to come back with something new. Something they'd never expect. *(Beat.)* Don't you think it's time? Don't you think it's time, Laurette? To get out of this apartment?

LAURETTE. And what? And do what?

EDDIE. Act.

LAURETTE. I'm afraid I've forgotten how.

EDDIE. Horseshit.

LAURETTE. Mr. Dowling!

EDDIE. That's horseshit and you know it. Don't make me court you, Laurette. I've got lots more important things to do than beg Laurette Taylor to do a play. But if it's begging you want, Laurie, I'll get on my knees-- *(Pulling out his handkerchief and begins to open it...)* I will get down on my knees--

LAURETTE. Don't be absurd--

EDDIE. *(Kneeling on the handkerchief.)* If that's what it's going to take to get you to say yes--

LAURETTE. Mr. Dowling--

EDDIE. Than begging you shall get!

(She laughs. Beat.)

EDDIE. Please, Laurette. You'll be magnificent.

LAURETTE. And if I disappoint you? What then?

EDDIE. It wouldn't be the first time I've been disappointed. And it most certainly wouldn't be the last. Disappointment is a fact of life.

LAURETTE. Maybe you should call Helen.

EDDIE. I don't want Helen, I want you. *(Beat.)* Sign the papers. Please sign the papers.

(Beat. She walks over to her vanity. The papers sit beneath a coffee mug. She lifts it.)

LAURETTE. It's stained--

EDDIE. It doesn't matter.

LAURETTE. But--

EDDIE. Sign them anyway.

LAURETTE. The coffee ring--

EDDIE. It adds character. Sign. *(Beat. She can't find a pen. He holds one out.)* Here.

(She takes it to the desk and signs. He walks over, takes the pen and the contract.)

EDDIE. Very well. I'll be out of your hair then. I know you've so very much to do.

LAURETTE. Wait--

EDDIE. And don't forget--

LAURETTE. Mr. Dowling--

EDDIE. The first rehearsal is next Tuesday! Start learning your lines, Amanda!

(Before she can speak, he exits. Beat. LAURETTE looks out at us and breaks the fourth wall.)

SECOND CONFESSION

LAURETTE. I learned a very valuable lesson this morning. If you want to walk, if you need to walk, to take your mind off something or someone or whatever it is that's ailing you you, you ought to wear something appropriate. A two mile walk in Central Park in your house slippers won't get you anything but blisters and carbuncles and a heckuva lot of stares. But when I left the apartment, I only planned to go up to the corner. To the liquor store. To My Man Harold. I'd walk in the door and My Man Harold would lean across that counter with a smile bright as a marquee and shout, "Hey, Miss T-" and I'd say, "My Man Harold!" And before I'd even tell him what I'd want, good old Harold would slide over a little bottle of whiskey. And I'd frown and he'd switch it out for a bigger one. That was our joke. Our schtick. Our routine for an invisible audience. A bunch of imaginary people I needed to prove something to. And My Man Harold, he'd add it to my monthly bill, and off I'd go, back up the street, and into my building and straight to the nearest empty glass. *(Beat.)* I missed him. Harold, I mean. But that walk to the corner felt so short. So, I just kept on walking. Another block, another four, another twelve, and into the park and across the park and past the Merry-Go-Round and just when my slippers were worn completely through I found myself back outside My Man Harold's little corner shop. *(Beat.)* But this time... This time I was just too tired to say hello.

SCENE 4

(The lights come to full burn. We are in the rehearsal room for THE GENTLEMAN CALLER. A Stage Manager, RANDOLPH ECHOLS is setting up chairs around a long table. There are scripts at every place and pencils all over. A jug of water and glasses sit at the center of the table.)

RANDOLPH. Early today, Miss Taylor?

LAURETTE. I'm always early. It's a tragic flaw.

RANDOLPH. A good one to have, though, that's for sure.

LAURETTE. And please, Laurette will be fine. There are only be four of us, after all.

RANDOLPH. Of course.

LAURETTE. And your name?

RANDOLPH. Randolph.

LAURETTE. Very well. Where shall I--

RANDOLPH. Right here. *(Sets down a chair.)* Mr. Williams asked that you sit with him.

LAURETTE. Oh. The--

RANDOLPH. Playwright. Yes.

LAURETTE. Did I read the papers right? Is his name really Tennessee?

STAGE MANAGER. Yes, ma'am.

LAURETTE. Ma'am won't do either.

STAGE MANAGER. Allright.

LAURETTE. Like the state.

STAGE MANAGER. Like the state.

LAURETTE. Tennessee.

(EDDIE DOWLING enters. He is dapper in a suit; flamboyant, handsome, charming and most certainly a narcissist.)

EDDIE. I can't believe it!

LAURETTE. Hello, Mr. Dowling.

EDDIE. I can't believe it, Laurie.

LAURETTE. Yes--

EDDIE. The Return of Laurette Taylor.

LAURETTE. It's only been five years.

EDDIE. Six, darling. Six since your last rendezvous with Dionysus.

(Beat.)

LAURETTE. Yes. Well. Everyone deserves a rest.

(MARGO JONES, a tall and fiercely intelligent woman with a thick Texan accent, enters with a younger actress, JULIE HAYDON. JULIE is shy, a lot like the character she'll soon be playing. But she is fiercely talented and always growing.)

MARGO. Eddie!

EDDIE. There she is.

MARGO. Eddie Dowling, as you live and breathe. It's as if I haven't seen you in--

EDDIE. 23 hours. And Julie, hello.

(JULIE nods and takes a seat.)

MARGO. I found her sitting outside on a bench!

EDDIE. Odd duck.

MARGO. She's just bashful. And you *are* an intimidating presence, Mr. Dowling. Give the girl a chance. And who's that? *(To LAURETTE.)* Laurie, hello!

LAURETTE. Hello.

(They embrace clumsily.)

MARGO. Oh, we are so happy to have you. How does it feel? Does it feel like home?

LAURETTE. It's a rehearsal studio, Margo. It feels like an empty room with lousy acoustics and too much light.

(Beat. After a moment, MARGO and EDDIE laugh, as if this were a joke.)

LAURETTE. And who is playing my son? Will I be meeting him, too?

EDDIE. That's me, Laurie!

LAURETTE. Aren't you the producer?

EDDIE. And the director.

MARGO. One of the directors.

LAURETTE. And you're playing my son.

EDDIE. Yes.

(Beat.)

LAURETTE. Opium dens indeed. *(To JULIE,)* And you must be playing my daughter.

JULIE. I am.

LAURETTE. Pretty girl. You can call me Laurie. Apparently everyone else already does. And we're missing someone else.

MARGO. Ah, yes. Mr. Ross.

EDDIE. Tony.

MARGO. Since The Gentleman Caller enters much later, we've asked him to come in after lunch.

EDDIE. We didn't so much ask as he insisted--

LAURETTE. And the playwright? I've yet to meet the man.

MARGO. Of course! He should be here any minute.

EDDIE. Tenn gets easily... distracted.

LAURETTE. It's a lovely play. Is he...

EDDIE. What?

LAURETTE. Young?

MARGO. Quite.

LAURETTE. The title, though--

(As they talk, TENNESSEE WILLIAMS lingers in the doorway unseen. 33, supremely handsome. Masculine and feminine at the same time. Charming but mysterious.)

MARGO. We've discussed it.

LAURETTE. It needs something.

EDDIE. He knows.

LAURETTE. A title should be magical. Grabbing. *(Beat.)* If the play is a world, or a house, or a-- a forest, then the title should be inviting. I'd like to visit Uncle Vanya's. He sounds like a nice man. *(Beat.)* It should invite us in.

TENNESSEE. Like the menagerie.

(Beat. Everyone looks at him.)

LAURETTE. Yes. *(Beat.)* Yes, the glass menagerie.

MARGO. Tennessee, hello.

TENNESSEE. Hello.

(RANDOLPH rushes to TENNESSEE'S side and ushers him to a chair next to EDDIE.)

RANDOLPH. Randolph Echols, Mr. Williams. I'm the Stage Manager. Anything you need--

EDDIE. *(Kissing his cheek,)* Darling.

TENNESSEE. Eddie... Go on, Miss Taylor. You were saying?

LAURETTE. Laurette will be just fine.

TENNESSEE. Go on.

LAURETTE. It all depends on where you want to take them. The audience. And once you've figured out, well, then it's easier to send the invitations, Mr. Williams.

TENNESSEE. Tenn. Please. Or Tennessee.

MARGO. It's quite a good idea.

TENNESSEE. Quite good indeed.

MARGO. Shall we start at the beginning?

TENNESSEE. Very well, then.

RANDOLPH. The Gentleman Caller.

(TENNESSEE clears his throat. RANDOLPH begins again.)

RANDOLPH. *The Glass Menagerie* by Tennessee Williams. Act One, Scene One.

(The lights pull back in on LAURETTE in pin-spot. She stands at her chair as the others freeze in position.)

THIRD CONFESSION

LAURETTE. It isn't the drink I miss the most. *(Beat.)* Sure, I liked the way it tasted. Nothing like a shot of whiskey down your throat on a cold New York morning. Nothing like it, no. Certainly don't miss the smell of it either. Used to like it fine but now the slightest whiff makes me sick to my stomach. It's the conversation. *(Beat.)* That's what I miss most. *(Beat.)* The stranger who is so lonely that knowing him makes you feel somehow LESS lonely. It's the smell of his cigarette. Even now, the smell of cigarette smoke makes me lonely. And loneliness makes me thirsty.

SCENE 5

(The lights reveal a cast deep in rehearsal. JULIE is crouched somewhere near LAURETTE. MARGO and the others sit stage left, TENNESSEE alone stage right, smoking a cigar. JULIE plays Laura a little too pathetically.)

JULIE/LAURA. "Has something happened, Mother?"

MARGO. Now, try another tactic--

JULIE/LAURA. "Mother, has something happened?"

LAURETTE/AMANDA. "I'll be all right in a minute, I'm just bewildered by life..."

JULIE/LAURA. "Mother, I wish that you would tell me what's happened!"

(Beat.)

LAURETTE/AMANDA. "As you know, I was-- *(Beat.)* As you know, I was supposed to be inducted into my office at the D.A.R. this afternoon. But I stopped off at-- *(Beat.)* I stopped at--" Excuse me. Could we--

MARGO. Yes?

LAURETTE. Could we go back?

JULIE. Was it the wrong cue?

EDDIE. You were right.

LAURETTE. It's just a little warm in here. I was distracted.

MARGO. Allright.

RANDOLPH. "Has something happened, Mother." Please.

(Beat. They reset.)

JULIE/LAURA. "Has something happened, Mother? Mother, has - something happened?"

LAURETTE/AMANDA. "I'll be all right in a minute, I'm just-- I'm just bewildered by life..."

JULIE/LAURA. "Mother, I wish that you would tell me what's / happened!"

TENNESSEE. *(Overlapping,)* Careful, Julie. Don't make her too-- May I, Margo? I'm sorry. *(MARGO nods.)* Don't make her pathetic. She's weak, not pathetic. She's delicate, not pathetic. Rose is delicate--

JULIE. Laura, you mean.

(Beat.)

TENNESSEE. Yes. *(Beat.)* Laura is delicate for a number of reasons. But there's one more important than all the others.

JULIE. Her legs.

TENNESSEE Sure. If you enjoy playing only the obvious.

JULIE. Her mother's criticism?

TENNESSEE. Is that a question?

JULIE No? *(Beat.)* No.

TENNESSEE. Laura is crippled, yes. And her mother certainly is a critical woman. And not to mention poor Laura probably gets sick a lot more than most girls her age. *(Beat.)* But it's isolation that's been her downfall. It's all that time she spends alone with her mind. A person shouldn't spend that much time with something as dangerous as their mind. I think that's where we lost-- that's HOW we lost-- *(Beat. He changes gears.)* There is more to Laura than delicacy and fear. You couldn't ask for a sweeter or more benign girl than her, or, in my opinion, one that's more of a lady. Laura is important like every one is important. But she's forgotten that fact. And that fact, Julie, is just as essential as vitamins. It's just as necessary as Scotch on a frosty January night. It's just as important as a-- *(Beat.)* As a brother's love.

LAURETTE. I believe you mean a *mother's* love, Mr. / Williams.

TENNESSEE. *(Sharply overlapping,)* I mean brother. A boy shouldn't go to the movies so much when his little sister needs him. Oh, boys will try to leave them behind. But they're more faithful than they intend to be. *(Beat.)* Selfish dreamer indeed. And Eddie?

EDDIE. Yes--

TENNESSEE. Don't think you can't judge him. Of course, you can!

EDDIE. But, Tenn, I really shouldn't--

TENNESSEE. You don't think he knows he's being selfish? You don't think Tom knows what he's done?

EDDIE. I think it might all be unconscious. Wouldn't that be easier to play?

TENNESSEE. It might very well be easier to play, Eddie, but it's not true. *(Beat.)* Try it again. Don't think too much about it, but-- Try again.

JULIE. Allright...

MARGO. Why don't we go back to the top of the page? Shall we?

RANDOLPH. Top of 23, please!

(The cast prepares and after a moment, they begin. JULIE is noticeably stronger in the role.)

JULIE/LAURA. "Has something happened, Mother? Mother, has - something happened?"

LAURETTE/AMANDA. "I'll be all right in a minute, I'm just-- I'm just bewildered by life..."

JULIE/LAURA. "Mother, I wish that you would tell me what's happened!"

(Beat.)

LAURETTE/AMANDA. "As you know, I was know, I was supposed to be-- I was supposed to be inducted into..."

(Beat.)

RANDOLPH. "...into my office at/ the D.A..."

LAURETTE/AMANDA. "I was supposed to be inducted into my office at the D.A.R. this afternoon. But I-- *(Beat.)* But..."

(Beat.)

RANDOLPH. "But I stopped off at Rubi--"

LAURETTE/AMANDA. "But I stopped off at Rubicam's business college to speak to your teachers about your-- About..."

RANDOLPH. "--your having a--"

LAURETTE/AMANDA. "--having a cold! And ask them-- *(Beat.)* Ask them-- *(Beat.)* I'm sorry. Margo, I'm sorry.

MARGO. Okay.

LAURETTE. It's just that--

MARGO. Allright. *(Beat.)* Julie, go and take five. Please.

(JULIE exits the room. The rest wait in silence, watching her as she goes. As soon as JULIE is gone, LAURETTE begins.)

LAURETTE. It's just-- It's been a long time and I've gotten a bit--

MARGO. I know.

LAURETTE. And it's so warm in here!

MARGO. Why don't you pick up the script and try to get through the rest of the scene?

LAURETTE. Well, if I haven't got it now, what makes you think I'll have it by opening?

MARGO. You're a terrific actress, Laurie. What makes this play any different?

LAURETTE. You wouldn't understand.

MARGO. Try me.

(Beat.)

TENNESSEE. First one cold? First one sober?

LAURETTE. In a long time, yes.

MARGO. But you feel--

LAURETTE. Strong? Yes. *(Beat.)* Mostly. But sometimes--

MARGO. Go on.

LAURETTE. Sometimes it's scary up here. This play, she's-- Amanda's--

MARGO. We all get scared, Laurette. But we haven't got any time for fear. *(Beat.)* If you don't think you're up to it, we'll understand. And we'll tell the press it's all a matter of scheduling.

TENNESSEE. Don't be absurd.

MARGO. I'm sorry?

TENNESSEE. It's a play. Nothing more, nothing less. Sure. She's a monster. They're all monsters. We're all monsters. Laurette Taylor didn't disappear from the stage because she was nice! Laurette Taylor disappeared because she'd turned into a monster. Feel free to tell me I'm wrong, Miss Taylor.

(Beat. She doesn't respond.)

TENNESSEE. I've woken up blind. Don't get me wrong, I have woken up blind. I have stumbled on my way to the bathroom. I have broken vases on my way to the door. I have broken windows when I can't see my keys. But sometimes things are good. You look around and things are *good*. Work? Good. Sex? Good. Food? Good. Bank account? Good. And if you're too blind to see all that good, then sweetie darling, you're wasting good liquor. And wasting liquor is a mortal sin. *(Beat.)* It's a monologue. It's not a noose. It's not an eviction notice, Laurie. It's a monologue. The only person pointing a deadly weapon at you is yourself. Get on with it so we can all go home.

(The door creaks open and JULIE pokes her head inside.)

JULIE. May I-- Is it time to--

TENNESSEE. Get on with it already. She's right there, Laurie.

LAURETTE. But--

TENNESSEE. Get on with it!

(LAURIE begins the monologue but is obviously overwhelmed. She gets through much of it, but the cracks in her surface show.)

LAURETTE/AMANDA. "As you know, I was supposed to be inducted into my office at the D.A.R. this afternoon. But I stopped off at Rubicam's business college to speak to your teachers about your having a cold and ask them what progress they thought you were making down there. I went to the typing instructor and introduced myself as your mother. She didn't know who you were. 'Wingfield', she said. 'We don't have any such student enrolled at the school!'"

MARGO. Good. Stop there. That's good.

(Beat.)

LAURETTE. I'm sorry.

TENNESSEE. There's nothing to be sorry about. But some of us have dinner reservations.

(He grabs his jacket and heads for the door, stopping to squeeze LAURETTE'S arm on the way out. Everyone watches him exit, silently amazed.)

EDDIE. Well!

MARGO. Allright. We'll stop here for today. Goodnight, everyone.

(Everyone exits as LAURETTE stands alone in pin-spot. At some point in the monologue, she should put on her coat and take her purse from the back of the chair.)

FOURTH CONFESSION

LAURETTE. Tenn was staring at me all through rehearsal. Waiting. Salivating. Wanting me to stumble or forget or belch or show even one little sign that I'd regressed, that I'd been drinking. Staring at me and sketching his next play. Figuring how he'd torture his next lonely Southern widow. He hates us, you know. Women. Reveres us, too, but punishes us. And that fucking cigar. It's all I see through rehearsal. It mocks me. That deep, red glow and it's Cheshire smile of smoke. *(Beat.)* Ever notice how liquor smells like smoke and smoke smells like liquor because every bar in America is hazy? Makes me thirsty when I'm up there. Makes me thirsty up there on Blue Mountain. But I got through it. I did. Up and over Blue Mountain and straight on through those Gentleman Callers, I got through. Sure, I was watching myself from the front row. Sure, I wasn't very good and oh, the notes, the notes, the man lives for notes. But I got through and I got in a cab and I came right back here and I made myself a cup of tea and sobbed when I took off my makeup and took a long, hard look at myself in the mirror. *(Beat.)* I could've had ten drinks. Twelve, if I tried hard enough. But instead, I put on my raincoat and went back outside - without an umbrella because what's the point of an umbrella when it's been raining for 8 long years - and I walked on up to the corner store and bought myself a cigar. Coughed my way through every little bit, but I got through it. I'll tell Tenn tomorrow. I smoked a Cahibo, I'll say. Aren't you proud of me? And maybe then that goddamn Cheshire smile won't bother me so much.

SCENE 6

(LAURETTE arrives at home. She clings to the script, which has yet to leave her hand. She takes a moment, surveys the apartment and sits on the arm of the couch.)

LAURETTE/AMANDA. *"Sometimes they come when they are least expected! Why, I remember one Sunday afternoon in Blue Mountain--"*

MARGUERITE *(off)*. Mom?

LAURETTE/AMANDA. *"One Sunday afternoon in Blue Mountain, your mother received seventeen gentlemen callers! Why, sometimes there weren't chairs enough to accommodate them all. We had to send--"*

(MARGUERITE enters from off-stage.)

MARGUERITE. Mama--

LAURETTE. Hello.

MARGUERITE. Why are you sitting there like that? And in your coat?

LAURETTE. I'm only just home a minute.

MARGUERITE. Take off your coat.

LAURETTE. I was thinking about a line. One of my lines in the play.

MARGUERITE. Allright.

LAURETTE. It is a very good play.

MARGUERITE. Just last week it was fine.

LAURETTE. Plays change.

MARGUERITE. People, too. Come on. Take off your coat. It's damp.

(MARGUERITE helps her mother out of the coat and hangs it on the rack.)

MARGUERITE. Have you eaten?

LAURETTE. No.

MARGUERITE. I'll make something.

LAURETTE. I'm not hungry.

MARGUERITE. You will be later.

LAURETTE. So, I'll make a little something.

MARGUERITE. But--

LAURETTE. I'm allright. *(Beat.)* I am. I'm allright.

MARGUERITE. It's just--

LAURETTE. What?

MARGUERITE. Margot rang. *(Beat.)* I suppose she was looking for you, but-- Rehearsal ended early.

LAURETTE. Yes.

MARGUERITE. You're awfully late.

LAURETTE. I went for a walk.

MARGUERITE. Where?

LAURETTE. Here and there.

MARGUERITE. Are you drunk?

LAURETTE. I went to a meeting, Marguerite. *(Beat.)* I was thirsty and frightened, so I went to a meeting and I got things off my chest.

(Beat.)

MARGUERITE. Dwight rang, too. Said he would see us on opening night. At the Civic in Chicago. *(Beat.)* He'll take the train.

LAURETTE. That will be nice.

MARGUERITE. We'll go to dinner. Somewhere fancy. And there'll be a party, too, I'm sure--

LAURETTE. Party?

MARGUERITE. Yes. Won't / there?

LAURETTE. *(Overlapping,)* I couldn't. Not yet.

MARGUERITE. Almost five years now. *(Beat.)* You're ready.

LAURETTE. That isn't for you to decide.

MARGUERITE. You'll want to celebrate.

LAURETTE. And neither is that.

(Beat. A long one.)

MARGUERITE. How about an omelette? That sounds good. I might even make one for myself...

LAURETTE. And coffee, too.?

MARGUERITE. And coffee too.

(MARGUERITE exits as the lights close in on LAURETTE again.)

FIFTH CONFESSION

LAURETTE. If I could run it through my veins, I would. *(Beat.)* It took a little while, but I have grown accustomed to the taste of coffee. When you try your first sip as a toddler, it surprises you. Looks rich and sweet. Like liquid chocolate. But then comes the bite. Almost chalky-like until you add the sugar. *(Beat.)* My daughter caught me adding ice cubes to my coffee the other day. I miss the sound they make against the glass, I told her. She didn't understand. *(Beat.)* The ice cubes frightened me. I'd be lying if I didn't say so. I was so desperate for the memory of a cocktail that I dropped the little bastards into my coffee cup and sipped away.

SCENE 7

(The lights rise on RANDOLPH who is crossing to LAURETTE. He hands her a few sheets of paper. This sequence should move quickly and at a high energy.)

LAURETTE. What are these?

RANDOLPH. Some new pages. *(Beat. He can see the terror in her eyes.)* Don't worry, Miss T. They're not so bad.

(EDDIE enters.)

EDDIE. Goooooood morning, everyone!

LAURETTE. Do you always do that?

EDDIE. What?

LAURETTE. Greet a small group like it's a big one? Like it's opening night at Grauman's?

EDDIE. I'm happy to be alive, darling. You should give it a try sometime.

(JULIE enters.)

RANDOLPH. *(Handing her the new pages,)* Miss Haydon, good morning.

JULIE. G'morning, Randy.

EDDIE. You've taken to calling him Randy now, have you?

JULIE. I asked him to call me Julie, but he--

RANDOLPH. Maybe once we get back to New York.

(MARGO enters, followed immediately by TENNESSEE. They quickly get into place for the beginning of a run-through, MARGO acutely aware of the ticking clock.)

MARGO. Good morning, everyone. Happy Tuesday!

LAURETTE Margo--

MARGO. Good morning, Laurie.

LAURETTE. These pages...

MARGO. We'll get to them.

LAURETTE. Will this be happening often?

TENNESSEE. As often as we need.

MARGO. We'll be running the entire show today. Our last rehearsal here in New York. Time certainly does fly. But first, let's take a look at the pages, please. Can everyone set for the top of page 18?

RANDOLPH. Tom says, "What do you think I'm at?"

EDDIE/TOM. "Aren't I supposed to have any patience to reach the end of, Mother?"

MARGO. Yes, thank you. Now, Tom, you'll be over here by the coat-rack. Right? Then you'll make your way over to the table--

LAURETTE. Margo, please--

MARGO. In a moment please, Laurette. And you'll, Eddie, you'll sit at your typewriter while Julie, honey, come over here... Thank you.

LAURETTE. This new bit here-- If we could just talk--

MARGO. Now, Laura will be setting the table around Tom's workplace. Don't cower too much, Julie, but be careful not to get involved in their argument. See?

JULIE. Yes.

LAURETTE. If I could just have one moment--

MARGO. *(Sternly,)* I really need quiet while we work, Laurie. Please. *(Beat.)* Thank you. Amanda will follow on "unimportant"--

RANDOLPH. "It seems unimportant to you, what I'm doing - what I want to do..."

MARGO. And here's where you can really let her out. Really sink those teeth into him.

LAURETTE. But will there always be so many new pages?

(Beat.)

MARGO. We will do our best to keep them at the minimum. But it's a new play and Tennessee is making new discoveries almost daily. *(Beat.)* May I keep moving forward now?

LAURETTE. Yes. (Beat.) Yes, I apologize.

MARGO. And you two will shout across the table. Tom, stage right of it and Amanda opposite. Laura, if you can scurry behind your mother... *(JULIE does.)* Good... To the far side of the couch-- *(She does.)* Exactly. Sit on the arm if you want. Watch, but don't engage. And Tom?

EDDIE. Mmm--

MARGO. Try coming closer to your mother right around Opium Dens. Allright? Back her up a little, maybe to the edge of the couch. *(They start to walk through it.)* Not too far, just a little! And stop halfway... Yes, good. At "dynamite", Tom will make his way back to the coat-rack--

(EDDIE walks through the scene as she explains.)

RANDOLPH. "My enemies plan to dynamite this place..."

MARGO. Exactly. And you'll drag it back behind you until you're standing in front of-- *(He is in front of LAURETTE again.)* Wonderful. Toss the coat aside and that's when you'll-- Yes. You'll hit the menagerie. Good. *(Beat.)* We'll let the moment settle a bit before Tom *bolts* out the fire escape. Does everyone understand?

LAURETTE. I follow him on...

RANDOLPH. "Unimportant."

LAURETTE. Right. *(Beat.)* Right. Thank you.

MARGO. Do we need to walk through that again, or can we start at the beginning?

LAURETTE. May I use my script?

MARGO. For the new pages, yes.

RANDOLPH. Set for the top, please, everyone!

(The cast scurries around to prepare for the run. TENNESSEE and LAURETTE steal a moment, unnoticed.)

LAURETTE. I smoked a Cahibo last night. In your honor.

TENNESSEE. You should've invited me. I would've liked to have seen that.

LAURETTE. Doesn't it ever make you lonely? Smoking?

TENNESSEE. The opposite. I find it comforting when my lips have a little company.

RANDOLPH. Places, please!

(Everyone else is set.)

TENNESSEE. Stay strong, Mrs. Wingfield. Blue Mountain isn't an easy one to climb.

(The run begins.)

EDDIE/TOM. "Yes, I have tricks in my pocket, I have things up my sleeve. But I am the opposite of a stage magician. He gives you illusion that has the appeal of truth. I give you--"

TENNESSEE. Appearance, Mister Dowling, not appeal.

MARGO. Tenn, please? Can you write it down for later?

TENNESSEE. What's the point of writing something down if it wasn't said correctly in the first place, Margo?

EDDIE. I'll get it.

TENNESSEE. I certainly hope so.

MARGO. Allright.

RANDOLPH. Back to the top, please.

(They reset. EDDIE begins again.)

EDDIE/TOM. "Yes, I have tricks in my pocket, I have things up my sleeve. But I am the opposite of a stage magician."

(As he speaks, the lights around LAURETTE fade to dark. It is a slow transition, almost as slow as the disappearance of EDDIE'S voice behind her own.)

EDDIE/TOM. "He gives you illusion that has the appeal of truth. I give you truth in the pleasant disguise of illusion. To begin with, /I turn back time. I reverse it to that..."

(LAURETTE is alone.)

SIXTH CONFESSION

LAURETTE. "I turn back time. I reverse it to that" August morning in 1912 when John brought in a script, all bound up in a bright red ribbon, and woke me up to share it. The pages were so crisp and clean. Pristine. And there it was in neat, black type. *Peg O' My Heart.* And just below, "For Laurette." *(Beat.)* Do you know? *(Beat.)* Do you know what it is to be loved like that? To be loved so hard you think your heart might explode? *(Beat.)* John had found himself quite the buyer, too. Mr. Morosco, can you believe it? Oliver Morosco. The play was good. Wonderful, really. But no one ever expected that sort of a sensation. Not even a man like Mr. Morosco. After all, it had been quite the year. For all of us, really. *(Beat.)* I'd just closed The Bird of Paradise. A dud. Only ran a few weeks. And would you believe? We closed just a day before another famous flop. I was cleaning out my dressing room while everyone was drowning. *(Beat.)* We lost friends, John and I. Three. They found one of them bobbing in the Atlantic. Never found the others, though. Still... Three funerals in one week. That was hard. My mouth was dry. So, I started with one. Just one before each funeral to-- To take off the edge, I told myself. And a person can get by on one a day for a long time. Years, really. A decade if you try hard enough. And I did. But when you measure a life in the theatre, you become awfully familiar with the sound of closing doors. And closing doors can make a person thirsty. And thirsty people drink. And when that Hollywood bastard cast Wanda fucking Hawley as Peg? John wouldn't have it. He fought while I drank. Fought so hard that cancer snuck in and ate him alive. *(Beat.)* So I poured myself another. *(Beat.)* And another. I'd drink anything. Anything at all. I would've bottled John's blood and drank that too if they'd let me. *(Beat.)* Tomorrow we leave for Chicago on the 20th Century. *(Beat.)* There they'll be in the dining car drinking their spirits. And there I'll be... Nursing mine. *(Beat.)* Do they have meetings like this one there? Are there basements in Chicago filled with people just like us? Will there be someone to talk to when the loneliness begins? Or will I stand there waiting? "Attempting to find in motion what was lost in space?" *(Beat.)* I think I've gone over my time. Thank you. For, uh-- for listening.

(Blackout.)

SCENE 8

(TENNESSEE is lying in bed, smoking in an open silk pajama top. Strangely enough, he looks a lot like Brick from Cat On A Hot Tin Roof, minus the cast. FRANK, his younger and equally attractive lover, is seated at the other side of the bed. He is removing his jewelry and changing for bed as they talk. FRANK sleeps in boxers, TENNESSEE in silk. Opposites certainly do attract.)

TENNESSEE. A bad rehearsal. Bad. And time so short. Poor old Laurette can't get her lines down. She fumbles and mumbles and practically nothing is done on interpretation, mood, inflection... It looks bad, baby.

FRANK. She'll get there.

TENNESSEE. When?

FRANK. Patience.

TENNESSEE. Haven't got any.

FRANK. Go down to the General Store and buy a little, then. She's an old lady. Compassion would look awfully nice on you.

TENNESSEE. It sounds like the Aunt Jemima Pancake Hour whenever she opens her mouth! The woman is ad libbing practically everything, Frank.

FRANK. Then fire her, Tenn. Call up Margo Jones right now and tell her to fire the woman. Just please let's not spend another hour of our lives talking about--

TENNESSEE. But doesn't it make sense? The old nothing who used to be a something?

FRANK. No one's a nothing, Tennessee. *(Beat.)* Even you know better than that.

(FRANK has finished changing for bed. He neatly folds his clothes over the back of a chair as a long silence passes between them. He switches off the lamp on his side of the bed, and climbs under the covers in silence. After a moment,)

FRANK. If you aren't going to read, then turn off the light.

TENNESSEE. What would I read?

FRANK. *The Lost Weekend* has been sitting on your nightstand for months. Either open it, or turn off the light.

TENNESSEE. Does it bother you?

FRANK. Yes.

TENNESSEE. I like a little light in the bedroom. Maybe it's time we get a nightlight. It lets me know I'm not alone. What's that Mrs. Darling says? "Dear night lights that protect my sleeping babes--" *(Beat.)* I can't remember the rest.

FRANK. "--burn clear and steadfast, tonight."

TENNESSEE. Oh, yes. That's it. Clear. And steadfast, too. *(Beat.)* If I write another play after this, I'd like it to be about a sick man. An invalid.

FRANK. A cripple.

TENNESSEE. No.

FRANK. What, then?

TENNESSEE. Emotional. An emotional cripple. *(Beat.)* I wonder if anyone has ever dealt with a more vicious and deadly opponent than have I with the beast in my nerves? I cannot kill him, nor ever entirely escape. I can only dodge. This I do with aplomb. With the most astonishing cunning. I've developed it. I've watched it grow. I've kept it safe. But the beast remains as he was: deadly, implacably malignant, treacherous... Huge. We've learned to coexist, this beast and I. *(Beat.)* Laurette and Amanda must learn to coexist. And where better to do that than inside all that loneliness? *(Beat. He looks to FRANK for an answer, but he has fallen asleep.)* A night-light would make the night a lot less lonely.

(TENNESSEE switches off his bedside lamp. Blackout.)

SCENE 9

(Deep in rehearsal on the stage of the Civic Theatre in Chicago, Illinois. The cast is only 2 days away from its first public performance. The environment is tense. TENNESSEE is not happy. In fact, he's volatile and explosive. The run-through is not going well.)

MARGO. Let's go back to the top of the page, please!

LAURETTE. I'm sorry--

MARGO. Don't be sorry, Laurette. No one has time for apologies. Top of the page.

(The cast resets.)

JULIE/LAURA. "It wasn't as bad as it sounds. I went inside places to get warmed up."

LAURETTE/AMANDA. "Inside where?"

JULIE/LAURA. "I went in the art museum and the bird-houses at the Zoo. I visited the penguins every day! Sometimes I did without lunch and went to the movies."

LAURETTE/AMANDA. "Selfish dreamer!"

RANDOLPH. Hold, please! *(Beat.)* Laura still has to talk about the Jewel Box, Miss Taylor.

TENNESSEE. And that isn't your line either. *(Beat.)* Your line, Laurette, is "You did all this to deceive me? Just for deception?"

LAURETTE. I know, Tenn. It's just--

TENNESSEE. We know. It's been a long time.

LAURETTE. That's not it.

TENNESSEE. It's warm in here.

LAURETTE. No--

TENNESSEE. What, then? The dust?

JULIE. The dust *is* dreadful.

TENNESSEE. You are not helping!

LAURETTE. I just... I'm--

TENNESSEE. My, oh, my, Laurette. "When you're disappointed, you get that awful suffering look on your face, like the picture of Jesus' mother in the museum!"

LAURETTE. That isn't fair!

TENNESSEE. Let's go, Mr. Echols. Back to the top of the page. Please!

MARGO. Tenn--

TENNESSEE. Keep moving forward, Margo. Please keep moving forward.

(The cast resets.)

JULIE/LAURA. "It wasn't as bad as it sounds. I went inside places to get warmed up."

LAURETTE/AMANDA. "Inside where?"

JULIE/LAURA. "I went in the art museum and the bird-houses at the Zoo."

LAURETTE/AMANDA. "You did all this to deceive me? Just--"

TENNESSEE. No, no, no!

LAURETTE. Please--

TENNESSEE. What? Please what?

LAURETTE. Please stop shouting!

TENNESSEE. I'm tense, Laurette! People shout when they are tense!

LAURETTE. Then please shout at the wall and not at me! When you shout, it frightens me. It distracts /me!

TENNESSEE. *(Overlapping,)* Distracts? I'm distracting!

MARGO. Tenn--

TENNESSEE. I suppose not knowing your lines doesn't distract Miss Haydon. Or Mr. /Dowling?

MARGO. *(Overlapping,)* Tennessee, please calm--

TENNESSEE. Or what about Mr. Echols? Do you think Mr. Echols will be able to follow in a script the actress is improving?

LAURETTE. You're being very cruel.

TENNESSEE. Writers are cruel, Miss Taylor. I would've thought you'd learned that by now.

LAURETTE. It isn't that I don't know the lines, /Mr. Williams--

TENNESSEE. *(Overlapping,)* Know them? Of course, you know them! You're just too damn scared to *say* them. And why? Too afraid to see yourself? Too afraid to see that poor old woman, that poor old, lonely woman staring back at you?

MARGO. I think you ought to go for a walk, Tenn. *(Beat.) Tom.*

(Beat.) Go for a walk.

TENNESSEE. You're right, Margo. Maybe if I go for a walk, Laurette Taylor will magically remember how to act.

(He exits. They watch him go. As soon as the door closes, MARGO continues.)

MARGO. I'm sorry, Laurette. You have to understand--

LAURETTE. I deserve it.

MARGO. It's very personal for--

LAURETTE. I'm holding everyone up.

EDDIE. I won't argue with that.

MARGO. Eddie!

LAURETTE. Aren't I though? *(Beat.)* Aren't I, Margot?

(Beat.)

MARGO. It's very personal for Tenn. *(With great care,)* He has invested a great deal--

EDDIE. We all have.

MARGO. --of him*self* into this play. His tragic flaw is "Caring Too Much". *(Beat.)* Should we take another stab at the scene?

LAURETTE. I'd like to go home for the evening. If that's allright with everyone, I'd like to go home.

EDDIE. But we haven't even gotten through the first act!

LAURETTE. Couldn't we start a little earlier tomorrow?

JULIE. I'm really rather worried about this--

MARGO. We're all tired. *(Beat. Defeated,)* It's allright, Laurette. We're all tired. Uh-- If Randolph could-- Can you find Anthony? Julie, do you mind if we stay to--

JULIE. Of course not!

RANDOLPH. He wasn't called until six.

MARGO. See if he can come in earlier.

RANDOLPH. Allright.

Tell him we'll work on his big scene with Laura. Julie, do you mind if we stay to--

MARGO

Very well. And Eddie--

EDDIE. I'm not going anywhere.

MARGO. Allright.

RANDOLPH. Miss Taylor, you're free to go.

(An uncomfortable beat. Everyone looks at LAURETTE.)

LAURETTE. Goodnight.

(The lights shift as LAURETTE steps into a pinspot. The others disappear into the darkness.)

SEVENTH CONFESSION

LAURETTE. Julie brought cough syrup to rehearsal yesterday. Says the theatre is so dusty it makes her cough. Such a DELICATE fucking flower. *(Beat.)* While they worked their way through a rather long stretch of scene, I sat directly across from the bottle of cough syrup and silently begged it to go away. Take a hike. Never come back. *Disappear.*

(A small glass of scotch appears by some kind of magic. In the original production, it was lowered from the ceiling, but you may have a different idea.)

LAURETTE CONT'D. If you could leave it there...? Yes! Thank you. *(Beat.)* I'd like to look at it for a while. Stare it down. Look it in the *eye*. If you see me reach for it, take it away! Before I drink it all, take it away. Before I fall back in love with all that bite, take it away! *(Beat. She watches the imaginary bartender leave, sits on the barstool and leans in close to speak to the drink in front of her.)* Hello, Old Friend. Remember me? Remember these eyes? Not so saggy anymore, huh? But all those lines, they don't just go away....

(A figure in silhouette appears behind her.)

LAURETTE. They stand proud like Redwoods. They hold their ground. *(Beat.)* We have that in common, my lines and I.

SCENE 10

(The figure steps into the light, as it grows around them.)

TENNESSEE. Are you going to drink that or leave it for a thirsty stranger?

(Startled, LAURETTE sees him for the first time. Beat. She hangs her head in shame and says nothing in return.)

TENNESSEE. May I?

(He takes the drink and swallows it all.)

TENNESSEE. If I hadn't come in just now--

LAURETTE. It would've stayed there. I wasn't here to-- to--

TENNESSEE. Drink.

LAURETTE. Right. I was here to test myself. To make sure I could do it. Just so I could be certain I wasn't wasting your time. So that I wouldn't disappoint anyone.

TENNESSEE. People disappoint themselves all the time, Laurette. It's a part of life.

LAURETTE. You're practically a baby. You'll see--

TENNESSEE. Oh, I've seen more than you might think. I've woken up in gutters. I've slept with men whose names I can't remember. I've destroyed another human being. I called that "Help". Would you believe it? Fought so hard to fix my poor little sister that when I tried to help her, I destroyed her. People disappoint themselves all the time. It's a part of life. Isn't it a part of yours?

LAURETTE. You know very well that--

TENNESSEE. And isn't it a part of Amanda's, too?

(Beat.)

LAURETTE. Yes.

TENNESSEE. She frightens you.

LAURETTE. So very, very much.

(Beat.)

TENNESSEE. You left us, Laurie. Just when we needed you most, you packed your things and you left us.

LAURETTE. I just needed a little time to think.

TENNESSEE. But nobody knew you were! You even pulled the telephone out of your hotel wall!

LAURETTE. A person needs quiet when they think! And nobody did any packing, Mr. Williams. My things are all still--

TENNESSEE. I'm not talking about packing clothes, Laurette! I am not talking about cigarettes or lipstick or perfumes. I'm talking about everything upstairs. All those demons we need you to battle.

(Other figures begin to appear in the shadows.)

TENNESSEE. Amanda Wingfield lives on the corner of Illusion and Reality. The only man who ever wanted her ran off at the first chance he got. There's a sort of denial there, don't you think? Just like there's a sort of a denial haunting you, Laurette... It's been haunting you for years. Any other woman would've taken down his picture if their man skips the light-fantastic out of town. But Amanda? Amanda leaves that picture there to remind herself of what was lost. She leaves it there and she lets it haunt her. *(Beat.)* And then there's her children. Oh, she lives her life through them. She perfects them. She polishes them.

MARGO/AMANDA. "Honey, don't push with your fingers. If you have to push with something--"

TENNESSEE. She trains them to be the perfect Southern creatures.

MARGO/AMANDA. "--the thing to push with is a crust of bread. And chew! Chew!

TENNESSEE. But then again, Laurette, wouldn't you? If you were that poor oppressed husband, wouldn't you run away? Now, Tom? Tom is her savior and her enemy. He is the remaining image of every man. Of every gentleman caller there wasn't.

EDDIE/TOM. "I haven't enjoyed one bite of this dinner."

TENNESSEE. And Laura is her burden. Oh, now Amanda doesn't really see it that way. But she is, isn't she? Just like Rose was--

LAURETTE. Rose?

TENNESSEE. My sister. *(Beat.)* Don't pretend as if you didn't know. Don't insult me.

LAURETTE. I didn't know. I

TENNESSEE. "She's a lovely girl."

MARGO/AMANDA. "It's rare for a girl as sweet an' pretty as Laura to be domestic!"

TENNESSEE. But sick. And terrified of her own shadow. If she even knows whose shadow it is... We did something terrible to her. We tried to fix her but we just wound up breaking her more. And poor little Laura? Oh, she hasn't even got a shadow to be scared of! Poor little Laura only wants to be loved and Amanda has just too much love to give. Amanda thinks she's trying to fix her, see?

MARGO/AMANDA. "But Laura is, thank heavens, not only pretty but also very domestic."

TENNESSEE. She passes the days by criticizing.

MARGUERITE/LAURA. "It isn't a flood."

TENNESSEE. She passes the hours by perfecting.

MARGUERITE/LAURA. "It's not a tornado, Mother."

TENNESSEE. She passes the years by picking them apart at the seams.

MARGUERITE/LAURA. "I'm just not popular like you were in Blue Mountain."

RANDOLPH/JIM. "You know what I judge to be the trouble with you? Inferiority complex!"

TENNESSEE. "Know what that is?"

RANDOLPH/JIM. "That's what they call it when someone low-rates himself."

TENNESSEE. They've been low-rain' themselves for years, The Wingfields! What's a person who low-rates himself supposed to do, Laurette? Hide?

JULIE/LAURA. "Oh, be careful!"

TENNESSEE. Cry?

MARGUERITE/LAURA. "If you breathe, it breaks!"

TENNESSEE. Run?

MARGUERITE/JULIE/LAURA. "Now, hold him over the light."

TENNESSEE. Drink himself to death?

ALL BUT LAURETTE. "You see how the light shines through him?"

LAURETTE. "It sure does shine!"

TENNESSEE. Or does he just keep telling himself all the lies he needs to hear? *(Beat.)* It's Blue Mountain that distracts from the boredom and emptiness of her living. It's Blue Mountain that's allowed her to let life pass her by. And it's Blue Mountain that's taught her to spend her days "attempting to find in motion what was lost in space." *(Beat.)* And what does she find? When the glass is empty, what does she finally find?

LAURETTE. Her reflection. *(Beat.)* Herself. *(Beat.)* Reflected back in all those little glass pieces.

(Beat.)

TENNESSEE. Go back to the hotel, Laurette. Go back to the hotel before your reflection changes.

(He throws a bill down on the bar and exits before she can respond. After a long moment, she grabs her purse and heads for the door. Blackout.)

SCENE 11

(A dressing room. It is Opening Night in Chicago. LAURETTE re-enters in her slip and robe, hair half done and sits at the table. She stares at herself in the mirror for a moment.)

LAURETTE. Hello, Mrs. Wingfield.

(After a moment of silent encouragement, she begins to apply her make-up. There is a knock at the door and MARGO is placing her head inside.)

MARGO. Hello, hello--

LAURETTE. Come in.

MARGO. Eddie too--

EDDIE *(off)*. Hello, Laurette!

LAURETTE. Come in, come in.

(They enter cautiously. Beat...)

MARGO. Are you...

LAURETTE. All set.

EDDIE. Are there any lines you'd like to--

LAURETTE. No.

(Beat.)

MARGO. It will be triumphant. Everyone has waited so long for this, Laurette. You've waited, too! *(Beat.)* It will be triumphant.

LAURETTE. I will aim for satisfactory. But of course I will accept triumphant.

EDDIE. If you need anything--

LAURETTE. Next door. I know, son.

(Beat.)

MARGO. Allright. Then we'll--

EDDIE. Yes... I'll--

LAURETTE. See you out there. *(Beat.)* Yes. *(They begin to exit.)* Oh, I--

MARGO. Yes?

LAURETTE. I was wondering. Is there a large audience?

EDDIE. Of course there is!

LAURETTE. Thank you.

EDDIE. Good show!

(EDDIE exits. MARGO hesitates a moment.)

MARGO. Take your time with the speeches if you have to. Every little piece of information is vital. And be sure to trust her. Amanda, I mean. There comes a point, Laurette, when an actress simply has to let the character do all the work.

LAURETTE. And the actress? What happens to her?

(Beat.)

MARGO. She disappears. *(With more sincerity than EDDIE,)* Good show, Laurette. *(Exits.)*

(LAURETTE turns back to the mirror and begins to apply her makeup. After a moment,)

LAURETTE. What would John say now? 61 years old and playing in Chicago...

(A knock at the door as MARGUERITE pokes her head inside. She has flowers.)

MARGUERITE. Mama--

LAURETTE. Margie, hello.

(LAURETTE rises. They hug.)

MARGUERITE. These are for you--

LAURETTE. Oh, lovely! I don't...

MARGUERITE. What?

LAURETTE. I don't have a vase.

MARGUERITE. Shall I go and--

LAURETTE. No, no. Stay. *(She drops in the water jug on her makeup table. They laugh. Beat.)* Would you mind...

MARGUERITE. What?

LAURETTE. Would you mind pinning up my hair? Ruby isn't here and I--

MARGUERITE. Of course.

(MARGUERITE grabs the pins off the dressing room table and gets to work.)

LAURETTE. Thank you, dear.

MARGUERITE. Did you call her?

LAURETTE. Helen Hayes scooped her up years ago. Bitch.

(They laugh for a moment. MARGUERITE points to a picture on the table.)

MARGUERITE. Is that...

LAURETTE. Your father.

MARGUERTE. And there's John, too. You keep them both on your table?

LAURETTE. Yes. I'm lost without them. Your father always knew the right lines to use.

MARGUERITE. And John?

LAURETTE. Oh... He knew all the cues.

MARGUERITE. Are you--

LAURETTE. Ready? I think so.

MARGUERITE. That isn't what I was going to ask.

(Beat.)

LAURETTE. Go on.

MARGUERITE. Are you thirsty?

LAURETTE. Every minute of every day.

MARGUERITE. I worry about you.

LAURETTE. I know.

MARGUERITE. I'm frightened for you.

LAURETTE. It's a play, Marguerite. It's not an eviction notice. It's a play. But it is a lot easier to get out there when you know the woman you're supposed to be playing. When you care for her. *(Beat.)* I think we have more in common than I realized.

MARGUERITE. Oh?

LAURETTE. Yes.

MARGUERITE. Tell me about her.

LAURETTE. It's a long story.

MARGUERITE. Tell me the short version.

LAURETTE. Well... At one she point loved herself. And then she started loving someone else. And when he went away, she had to find something else to love. And once she found it, she couldn't let go.

(Beat.)

MARGUERITE. Sounds like she just wanted something to help pass the time.

LAURETTE. Isn't that all we ever want?

(A knock on the door. From off, we hear...)

RANDOLPH *(off)*. 10 minutes, Miss Taylor!

LAURETTE. Thank you.

MARGUERITE. I should get to my seat.

LAURETTE. Are the pins in tight?

MARGUERITE. Yes. *(Beat.)* You'll be wonderful. Dwight's here too. He wanted to wait until after but I--

LAURETTE. *(With great sincerity,)* Thank you, Marguerite..

MARGUERITE. It's just hairpins.

LAURETTE. No, silly. Not the pins.

(Beat.)

MARGUERITE. Mom--

LAURETTE. I know. Go sit down. I've got a play to do.

(MARGUERITE and her mother touch foreheads. It's a quiet, gentle gesture. After a moment, she exits. LAURETTE looks back at herself in the mirror.)

LAURETTE. It's time.

(She removes her robe and stands in her slip. There is a knock at the door as TENNESSEE peeks his head inside. LAURETTE quickly grabs Amanda's iconic dress and covers herself in it,

suddenly a demure Southern woman. She has transformed into AMANDA. LAURETTE is gone. The accent is thick. Molasses.)

LAURETTE/AMANDA. Go away, please!

TENNESSEE (Poking his head inside,). Laurette, it's--

LAURETTE/AMANDA. Not now, sir! Go away.

TENNESSE. I only wanted to-

LAURETTE/AMANDA. I asked you not to enter, Mr. Williams.

(Beat.)

TENNESSEE. Allright.

AMANDA. A woman needs her privacy.

TENNESSEE. Allright...

AMANDA. She deserves it.

TENNESSEE. Yes. *(Beat.)* You do look lovely.

AMANDA. This? It's a simple frock.

TENNESSEE. It suits you.

AMANDA. A man of your age shouldn't flirt with a woman of mine, Mr. Williams.

TENNESSEE. But--

AMANDA. I know when a gentleman is flirting.

(A long beat. He suddenly understands.)

TENNESSEE. Well. I just couldn't help myself, Mrs. Wingfield.

Good evening.

(Beat. He nods to her and goes. She turns away from the door and catches her reflection in the mirror. She studies herself for a long while. And then,)

AMANDA. What happened to you, Amanda?

(A knock, quickly followed by,)

RANDOLPH *(off)*. Places please, Miss Taylor.

(Beat. She doesn't respond. He cracks open the door.)

RANDOLPH. Miss Taylor?

LAURETTE. *(Startled,)* Yes?

RANDOLPH. Places?

LAURETTE. Oh.

RANDOLPH. Places for the top of the show.

LAURETTE. Yes, Randolph. Places. Thank you.

RANDOLPH. Good show.

(He exits. She takes one last look at herself in the mirror and exits out the door, striking the switch on her way out. Blackout..)

FINAL CONFESSION

(A pool of light appears onstage. TENNESSEE enters and steps into it.)

TENNESSEE. I didn't realize it til much later, but it wasn't Laurette Taylor I'd wished a good show. You see, she'd become somebody else. Everyone said she could. That she'd done it before and she would do it again. It is not necessary to mention the mistaken reservation some people had about her ability to remain long with a play. But Laurette was painfully aware of it and she worked hard to beat it. No, that wasn't Laurie in the dressing room, that was-- that was Amanda Wingfield. *(Beat.)* Wasn't it? Wasn't that my Amanda? *(Beat.)* I've told a lot of people that there's a lot of me in Tom. But I never really told anyone just how much of Amanda's loneliness sits right here... *(He touches his breast bone.)* Right here like a boulder on my chest. And not just loneliness, but desperation too. And bitterness. Oh, and anger! Certainly anger. Cause when you get desperate, you get angry. And when I get angry, I get thirsty. Oh, and not just thirsty, but I like pills, too. I'm a mess, my dears. Oh, I am a mess but at least there is desire to find all the things I've lost. *(Beat.)* But basements with stale coffee and uncomfortable chairs and unflattering lighting are not exactly my ideal setting. No. So I stand here now with reluctance. *(Beat. The lights in the audience should build as the fourth wall falls.)* Today is December 8th. The year is 1946. I have been sober for 24 hours. Laurette Taylor died yesterday. A heart attack, I do believe. In that unfathomable experience of ours there were sometimes hints of something that lied outside the flesh and its mortality. Together, we searched for what was lost in the menagerie. In her's. In mine. *(Beat.)* The first time Laurette played Amanda in front of an audience was the first time I promised myself I would be sober again someday. I have promised myself that many times. 500 performances. Maybe more. Somewhere along the way, I lost count. But Laurette.... Well.... *(Beat.)* If Laurette Taylor could do that after goin to Hell and back like I'm doin' now and I'm sure I'll do again? *(Beat.)* There just might be hope for life yet. *(He is interrupted.)* Oh. I do believe I have gone over my time. I thank you. Thank you for listening.

(TENNESSEE walks to an empty seat in the house. A beat. He takes a deep breath and... Blackout. End of play.)

WHAT WAS LOST

ACKNOWLEDGMENTS

Writing this play would not have been possible without the Notebooks of Tennessee Williams, painstakingly edited by Margaret Bradham Thornton. In addition, the feedback of all of the actresses, directors and designers who have worked on this play was immeasurable in the process.

Great thanks to Georganne Guyan Bender, Charles Busch, Robert Featherstone, Irma and Sol Gurman, Julie Halston, James Horan, Lucille Kenney, Rich Kizer, JoAnn Mariano, Patti Mariano, Dale McCausland, Polly McKie, Samantha Mercado-Tudda, Carey Purcell and Celia St. John for their unwavering support and encouragement.

Overwhelming gratitude to Albert J. Pica, Theresa Pica, Susan Percoco and Steve McCasland.

ABOUT THE AUTHOR

Steven Carl McCasland is the founder and Artistic Director of The Beautiful Soup Theater Collective. A Pace University graduate, Steven's critically acclaimed plays have been seen in New York and Bermuda. In 2009, Steven was commissioned to adapt poet Jack Wiler's anthologies into a solo performance about Wiler's struggle with HIV. That play, *Fun Being Me*, was workshopped with Jack in the title role before his passing in 2009. Steven's other plays include: *When I'm 64, Hope & Glory, Opheliacs Anonymous, Blue, Pulchritudinous,* Huntington Award in Playwriting - First Place), and *Billy Learns About Captain Kirk* have all received productions regionally and in Manhattan. In June of 2011, Steven premiered his original adaptation of Lewis Carroll's *Alice's Adventures in Wonderland*. Setting Wonderland in the heart of Paris, he also directed and was featured in the cast as the Mock Turtle. After its one week workshop, *Alice Au Pays Des Merveilles* was picked up for an extended run at The SoHo Playhouse through September. His acclaimed play *neat & tidy* made a splash on the Bowery in May of 2012, with critics hailing McCasland as a new Thornton Wilder and the play as one of the Top Dramatic Plays of the year. After critically acclaimed workshops of Steven's plays *Little Wars* and *What Was Lost* in 2014, Beautiful Soup partnered with The Clarion Theatre to present five of his plays in repertory. Those five plays began on May 7th, 2015 and ran through the end of the month. Also featured in rep were *28 Marchant Avenue, Der Kanarienvogel (The Canary)* and a revival of *neat & tidy*. His writing has been acclaimed by New York critics as "brilliant", "riveting", "mesmerizing" and "extraordinary".

Made in the USA
Middletown, DE
23 October 2024